JUMPIN' J UKULELE beach party

Compiled and Arranged by Jim Beloff

SONGS

Copyright © 2001 FLEA MARKET MUSIC, INC.
Box 1127, Studio City, CA 91614

7777 W. BLUEMOUND RD. P.O. BOX 13819 MILWAUKEE, WI 53213

Edited by Ronny S. Schiff
Cover and Art Direction by Elizabeth Maihock Beloff
Graphics and Music Typography by Charylu Roberts

Surf's Up!

Thanks to its association with Hawaii, the ukulele seems particularly at home on the beach. The original beachboys of Waikiki were uke players and early pictures of the California surf scene always include a uke or two. Maybe it's no coincidence that many of the most famous songs about the beach, surfing and summer play especially well on the ukulele.

Ever since the publication of *Jumpin' Jim's '60s Uke-In*, we've been on the lookout for more pop songs to arrange for ukulele. While it is possible to play virtually anything on the uke, some songs seem born to be strummed. The chords to "Surfer Girl" are especially uke-friendly, as are many of Brian Wilson's Beach Boys' songs. In this songbook we are happy to include a number of Brian's tunes as well as other beach and summer hits. Also part of the surf sound were the many instrumentals that were popular during the heyday of the '60s. While these often featured reverb-drenched electric guitars, we felt it wouldn't be a beach party without uke versions of "Wipe Out" and "Misirlou." In the case of "Misirlou," it was a delight to discover that the man who made it famous, the "King of the Surf Guitar," Dick Dale, had started his fretted musical career on the humble ukulele. He kindly shares his story here, admitting, "if it wasn't for the uke… I wouldn't be Dick Dale."

We are also thrilled to include the West Coast classic "26 Miles," which, according to songwriter Bruce Belland, was written on a uke. The original lyric includes a reference to a guitar, but for this songbook, Bruce wrote a special set of ukulele-themed lyrics.

There are many fine folks who helped in the creation of this songbook. Many thanks to the audition night gang of Peter Wingerd, Mimi Kennedy, Larry Dilg, Gene Sculatti, Peter Thomas and Ronny Schiff. Swagerty Kooky-Ukes information courtesy of Keith Bramer, Fred Swegles and, especially, Kitty Jones. Mahalos also to the Hawaiian Surf Club of San Onofre, Alan Yoshioka, Daniel Fujikake and Hillel Wasserman. Finally, major thanks to Dick Dale and Bruce Belland as well as Jumpin' Jim's regulars, Charylu Roberts, Wendy Dewitt and my "beach bunny" Leapin' Liz. See you on the beach!

—Jumpin' Jim Beloff
Los Angeles, CA 2001

Also Available: (Books) *Jumpin' Jim's Ukulele Favorites; Jumpin' Jim's Ukulele Tips 'N' Tunes; Jumpin' Jim's Ukulele Gems; Jumpin' Jim's Ukulele Christmas; Jumpin' Jim's '60s Uke-In; Jumpin' Jim's Gone Hawaiian; Jumpin' Jim's Camp Ukulele; Jumpin' Jim's Ukulele Masters: Lyle Ritz; The Ukulele: A Visual History.* **(CDs)** *Jim's Dog Has Fleas; For The Love Of Uke; Legends Of Ukulele; It's A Fluke.* **(Video)** *The Joy Of Uke.*

For all inquiries: Flea Market Music, Inc., Box 1127, Studio City, CA. 91614.
Visit us on the web at www.fleamarketmusic.com

How To Use This Book

Tuning

The smallest and most popular size of the ukulele is the soprano. All of the songs in this book were arranged for the soprano ukulele in C tuning. Nonetheless, if you tune any sized uke as shown below, you will be able to play the chords as written.

The easiest way to tune the ukulele is with a pitch pipe, matching the strings with the notes:

This corresponds to that famous melody:

Here are the notes on the keyboard:

Tablature Arrangements

Three of the songs included in this collection ("Misirlou," "Wipe Out" and parts of "Help Me Rhonda") feature tablature arrangements. These arrangements show both the melody on the staff, uke chord grids above, and ukulele tablature that tells you which strings should be played at which frets. The four lines of the staff correspond to the four strings of the uke, first string at the top, and the numbers written on the lines indicate which frets should be fingered. The numbers in the tablature should be played in the same rhythm shown in the staff above. If numbers are stacked on top of each other they should be played simultaneously as a chord.

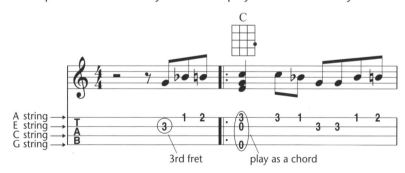

For More Information

For additional tips on playing the ukulele refer to the method and songbook, *Jumpin' Jim's Ukulele Tips 'n' Tunes* (Flea Market Music) and video, *The Joy Of Uke* (Homespun Tapes).

DiCK DALE: Where It All Began

King Of The Surf Guitar, Dick Dale shares with us how it all began on a ukulele

Back when I was in elementary school in Quincy, Massachusetts—I was born May 4th, 1937—I listened to my Dad's records of the Big Band era. That's why I learned to play drums like Gene Krupa—that's how I got my rhythm. I used to beat knives on my mother's cookie and flour canisters, and my father would whack me every time he came home because I chipped all the canisters. We did not have money. I used to work for 5 cents an hour in an Arabic bakery, and then I would work setting up bowling pins—so where are you going to get the money to buy stuff?

I was reading the back of a Superman magazine, and it said, "Sell [so many] jars of Noxema Skin Cream and we'll send you this beautiful ukulele," which was green and had a cowboy rearing on his horse, twirling a lariat over his head. To me, that was so cool. I went out every night in the snow—back there it snowed so hard you couldn't open the doors—I had to climb out of a window to go to school. I would say, "Mom, I gotta sell these things" and I would bang on the [neighbor's] doors—it was nighttime, it was dark, and I'd say, "Mrs. Freel would you please buy some Noxema Skin Cream?" "Dicky, Dicky, what are you doing out in the middle of the night? Get back home where you belong in bed!" "I gotta sell this Noxema Skin Cream so I can buy a ukulele." They felt sorry for me. (In fact, to this day I still shave with Noxema Skin Cream.)

I sold enough, about forty dollars worth, sent it away, and waited and waited and waited—over a month went by. Finally the ukulele came and I was so excited. I opened up this cardboard package, and there was this painted green ukulele. I was so dejected, because it was made out of particle cardboard with black pegs pushed into the holes in the back of the neck; so when you tried to turn the catgut strings the pegs would just fall right out of the back. I was so frustrated and upset, I smashed it in the garbage can. So I got my little Red Rider wagon and collected every soda bottle I could find. Then I walked a couple of miles to the store up the road in the snow pulling these damn bottles in my wagon. I got about six dollars.

Then I walked seven miles into the town where there was a little music store and they sold me my first plastic ukulele for five dollars and ninety five cents. It was brown on the bottom and cream on the top, and the pegs had screws in them so they wouldn't fall out. That was my first ukulele.

Now I went and got a Chordmaker—I didn't know how to make a chord. I strapped it on my ukulele and it would push down the strings for a C or G chord. But when I strummed it, it would just rattle and it was such a horrible sound I took the Chordmaker off and I bought this book. The book said, "put your finger here and here and here to make a G, and here and here and here to make a D, and here's how to make a C." It was just three chords I was trying to learn. I couldn't understand why my fingers would not go there because the book didn't say "turn it around, stupid, you're left-handed! Hold it the other way."

I never realized that all my rhythm from playing the knives to the Gene Krupa and Harry James records was coming out of my left hand. I automatically held the ukulele upside down and backwards. So here I was trying to make a chord backwards. I just kept stretching my fingers with my other hand, bending them, and I would hold them there. I got so frustrated I used this sticky old electrician's tape to hold my fingers down and I'd go to sleep that way. And that's how I made my first three chords, and the first song that I ever learned [on the uke] was the "Tennessee Waltz."

Not long after, Dick had an opportunity to buy his first guitar for $7. When he asked how to play it the seller suggested he play the four higher strings that most resembled ukulele tuning and ignore the two low ones, which he did... for a while, anyway.

**"If is wasn't for the uke...
I wouldn't be Dick Dale."**

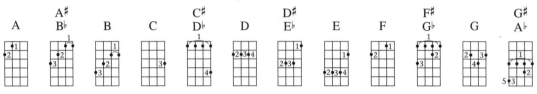

Chord Chart

Tune Ukulele
G   C   E   A

MAJOR CHORDS

A | A♯ B♭ | B | C | C♯ D♭ | D | D♯ E♭ | E | F | F♯ G♭ | G | G♯ A♭

MINOR CHORDS

Am | A♯m B♭m | Bm | Cm | C♯m D♭m | Dm | D♯m E♭m | Em | Fm | F♯m G♭m | Gm | G♯m A♭m

DOMINANT SEVENTH CHORDS

A⁷ | A♯⁷ B♭⁷ | B⁷ | C⁷ | C♯⁷ D♭⁷ | D⁷ | D♯⁷ E♭⁷ | E⁷ | F⁷ | F♯⁷ G♭⁷ | G⁷ | G♯⁷ A♭⁷

DOMINANT NINTH CHORDS

A⁹ | A♯⁹ B♭⁹ | B⁹ | C⁹ | C♯⁹ D♭⁹ | D⁹ | D♯⁹ E♭⁹ | E⁹ | F⁹ | F♯⁹ G♭⁹ | G⁹ | G♯⁹ A♭⁹

MINOR SEVENTH CHORDS

Am⁷ | A♯m⁷ B♭m⁷ | Bm⁷ | Cm⁷ | C♯m⁷ D♭m⁷ | Dm⁷ | D♯m⁷ E♭m⁷ | Em⁷ | Fm⁷ | F♯m⁷ G♭m⁷ | Gm⁷ | G♯m⁷ A♭m⁷

MAJOR SIXTH CHORDS

A⁶ | A♯⁶ B♭⁶ | B⁶ | C⁶ | C♯⁶ D♭⁶ | D⁶ | D♯⁶ E♭⁶ | E⁶ | F⁶ | F♯⁶ G♭⁶ | G⁶ | G♯⁶ A♭⁶

MINOR SIXTH CHORDS

Am6 A#m6/B♭m6 Bm6 Cm6 C#m6/D♭m6 Dm6 D#m6/E♭m6 Em6 Fm6 F#m6/G♭m6 Gm6 G#m6/A♭m6

MAJOR SEVENTH CHORDS

Amaj7 A#maj7/B♭maj7 Bmaj7 Cmaj7 C#maj7/D♭maj7 Dmaj7 D#maj7/E♭maj7 Emaj7 Fmaj7 F#maj7/G♭maj7 Gmaj7 G#maj7/A♭maj7

DOMINANT SEVENTH CHORDS WITH RAISED FIFTH (7th+5)

A7+5 A#7+5/B♭7+5 B7+5 C7+5 C#7+5/D♭7+5 D7+5 D#7+5/E♭7+5 E7+5 F7+5 F#7+5/G♭7+5 G7+5 G#7+5/A♭7+5

DOMINANT SEVENTH CHORDS WITH LOWERED FIFTH (7th-5)

A7-5 A#7-5/B♭7-5 B7-5 C7-5 C#7-5/D♭7-5 D7-5 D#7-5/E♭7-5 E7-5 F7-5 F#7-5/G♭7-5 G7-5 G#7-5/A♭7-5

AUGMENTED FIFTH CHORDS (aug or +)

Aaug A#aug/B♭aug Baug Caug C#aug/D♭aug Daug D#aug/E♭aug Eaug Faug F#aug/G♭aug Gaug G#aug/A♭aug

DIMINISHED SEVENTH CHORDS (dim)

Adim A#dim/B♭dim Bdim Cdim C#dim/D♭dim Ddim D#dim/E♭dim Edim Fdim F#dim/G♭dim Gdim G#dim/A♭dim

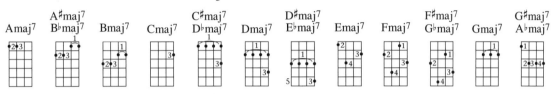

7

Blue Moon

Words by
LORENZ HART

Music by
RICHARD RODGERS

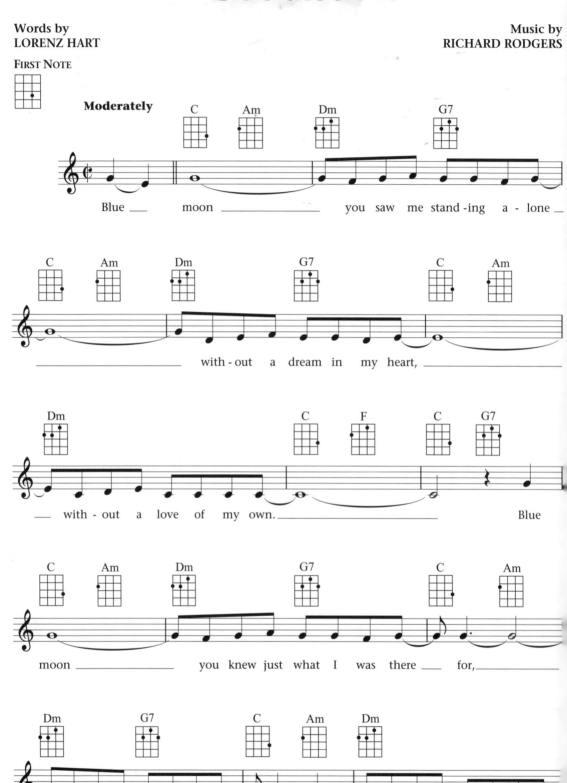

Blue __ moon _____ you saw me stand -ing a - lone _

_____ with - out a dream in my heart, _____

__ with - out a love of my own. _____ Blue

moon _____ you knew just what I was there __ for, _____

__ you heard me say -ing a pray'r __ for _____ some - one I real -ly could care

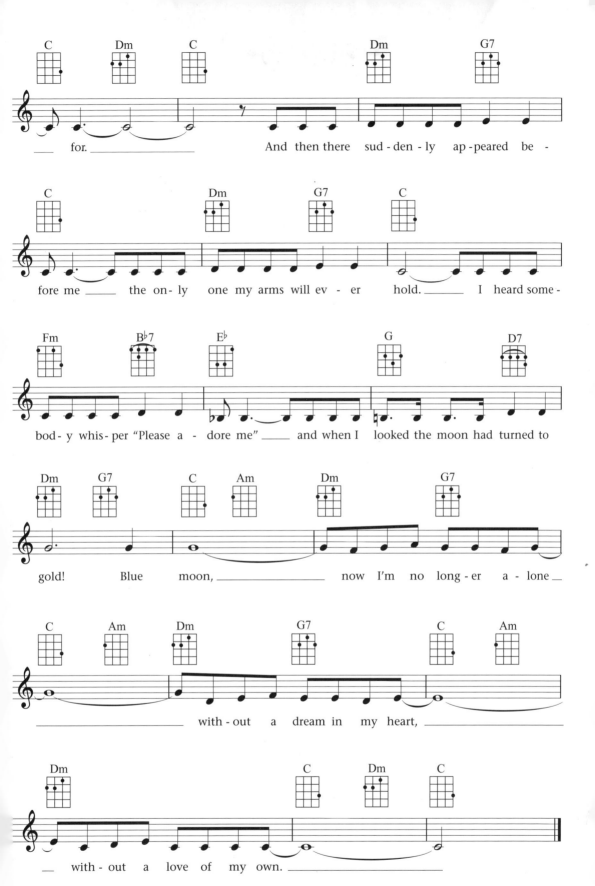

California Girls

Words and Music by
BRIAN WILSON and MIKE LOVE

FIRST NOTE

1. Well, East Coast girls are hip, I real-ly dig those styles they wear; _____ and the South-ern girls _____ with _____ the way they talk, _____ they knock me out when I'm down there. _____ The Mid-west farm-ers' daugh-ters real-ly make you feel all right, _____ and the North-ern girls _____ with _____ the way they kiss, _____ they keep their

2. West Coast has the sun-shine, and the girls all get so tanned; _____ I dig a French bi-ki-ni on Ha-wai-ian is-lands, dolls by a palm tree in the sand. _____ I been all a-round this great big world, and I've seen all kinds of girls, _____ but I could-n't wait _____ to _____ get back in the States. _____ Back to the

boy - friends warm at night. ⎱
cut - est girls in the world. ⎰

I wish they all could be

___ Cal - i - for - nia girls, _____ I
(I wish they all could be ___ Cal - i - for - nia girls,)

wish they all could be ___ Cal - i - for - nia girls. _____ 2. The

girls. _____

I wish they all could be ___

Repeat and Fade

___ Cal - i - for - nia girls, _____ I
(I wish they all could be ___ Cal - i - for - nia;)

Heatwave
(Love Is Like A Heatwave)

Words and Music by
EDWARD HOLLAND, LAMONT DOZIER
and BRIAN HOLLAND

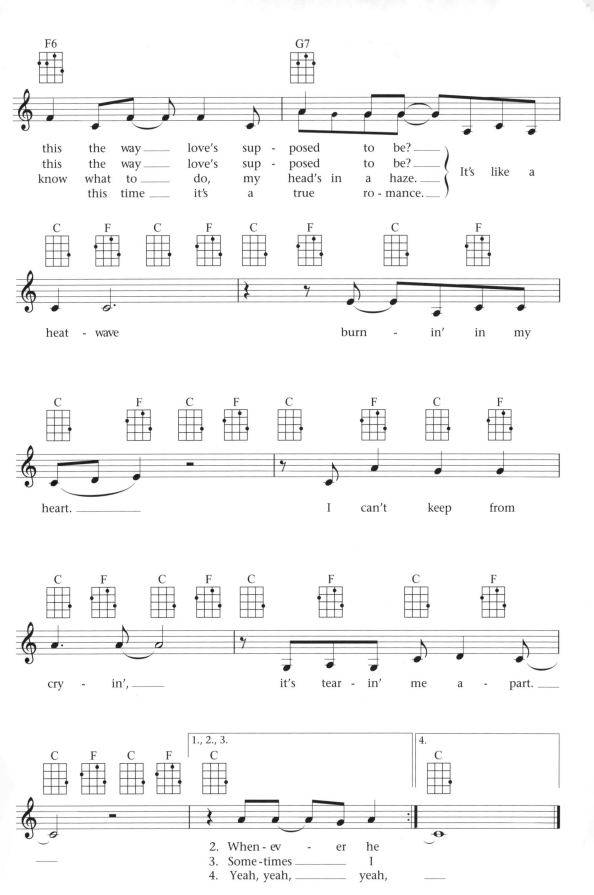

this the way ___ love's sup - posed to be? ___
this the way ___ love's sup - posed to be? ___
know what to ___ do, my head's in a haze. ___
this time ___ it's a true ro - mance. ___
It's like a

heat - wave   burn - in' in my

heart. ___   I can't keep from

cry - in', ___   it's tear - in' me a - part. ___

1., 2., 3.

2. When - ev - er he
3. Some - times ___ I
4. Yeah, yeah, ___ yeah, ___

4.

Help Me Rhonda

Words and Music by
BRIAN WILSON and MIKE LOVE

1. Since she put me down I've been out do-in' in my head, ___ come in late at night ___ and in the morn-in' I just lay in bed. ___ Well,
2. gon-na be my wife and I was gon-na be her man, ___ But she let an-oth-er ___ guy come be-tween us and it ruined our plans. ___ Well,

Rhon-da you look ___ so fine, ___ and I know it would-n't take much time, ___ for you to help me, Rhon-da, help me get her out of my heart.

Rhon-da you caught ___ my eye, ___ and I'll give you lots of rea-sons why, ___ you got-ta

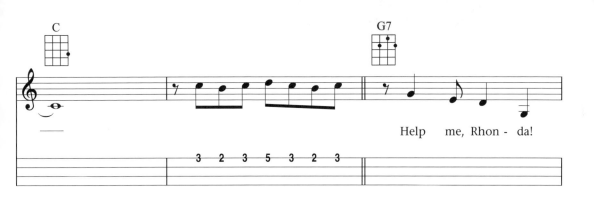

Help me, Rhon - da!

Help, help me, Rhon - da! Help me, Rhon - da! Help, help me, Rhon - da!

Help me, Rhon - da! Help, help me, Rhon - da! Help me, Rhon - da!

Help, help me, Rhon - da! Help me, Rhon - da! Help, help me, Rhon - da!

Help me, Rhon - da! Help, help me, Rhon - da! Help me, Rhon - da!

G7   No chord   **1.** C

Yeah, get her out of my heart. ___   2. She was

```
3 3 3 0              3 3 3 0
        0  3  3 1 0          0  3  3  1  0
```

2. C   G7

Help   me, Rhon - da!

C

Repeat and fade out

Help, help me, Rhon - da!   Help me, Rhon - da!   Help, help   me, Rhon - da!

In The Summertime

Words and Music by
RAY DORSET

FIRST NOTE

With a Steady Beat

1. In the sum-mer-time, ___ when the weath-er is high, ___ you can
2. dad-dy's rich, ___ take her out for a meal. ___ If her
(D.C.) When the win-ter's here, ___ yeah, it's par-ty-time. ___ Bring a

stretch right up ___ and ___ touch ___ the sky. ___ When the
dad - dy's poor, ___ just ___ do what you feel. ___ Speed a -
bot - tle, wear your bright clothes, it - 'll soon be sum-mer-time and we'll

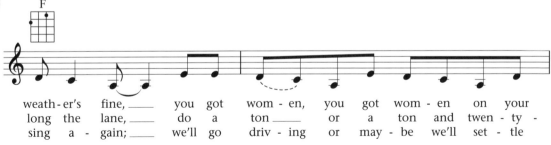

weath-er's fine, ___ you got wom-en, you got wom-en on your
long the lane, ___ do a ton ___ or a ton and twen-ty -
sing a - gain; ___ we'll go driv-ing or may-be we'll set-tle

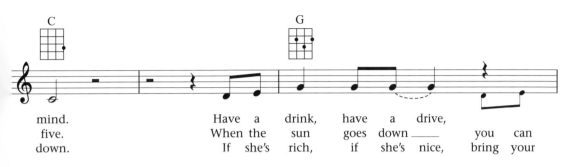

mind. Have a drink, have a drive,
five. When the sun goes down ___ you can
down. If she's rich, if she's nice, bring your

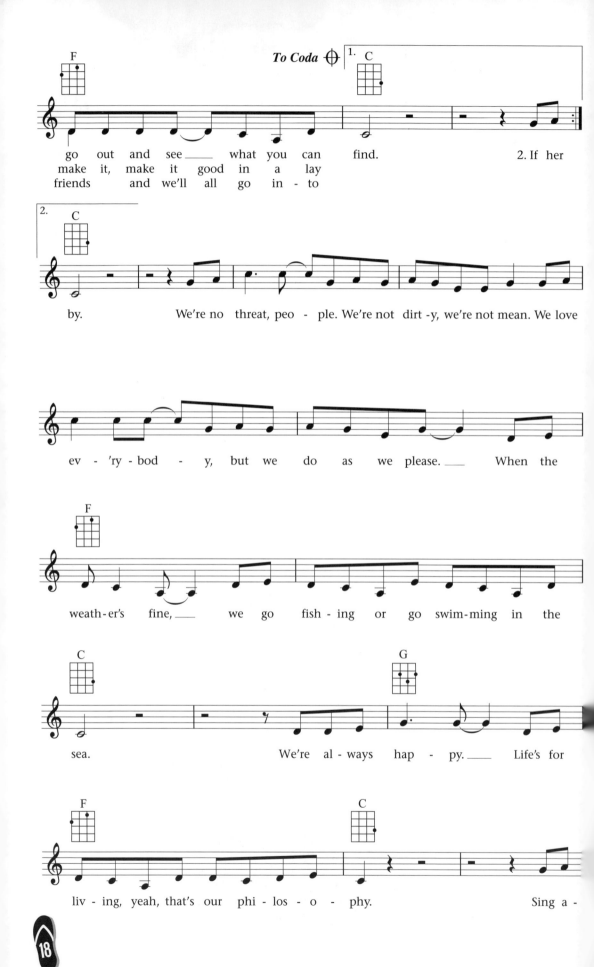

long with us, ___ dee dee dee dee dee. ___ Dah do dah dah dah. ___ Yeah, we're

F

hap-hap - py. ___ Dah dah ___ dah, dee dah do dee do do dah do

C

G

dah. Dah do dah dah dah ___

F

C

D.C. al Coda

⊕ *Coda*

C

dah dah dah ___ do dah dah. ___ town.

I'll Remember You

Words and Music by
KUI LEE

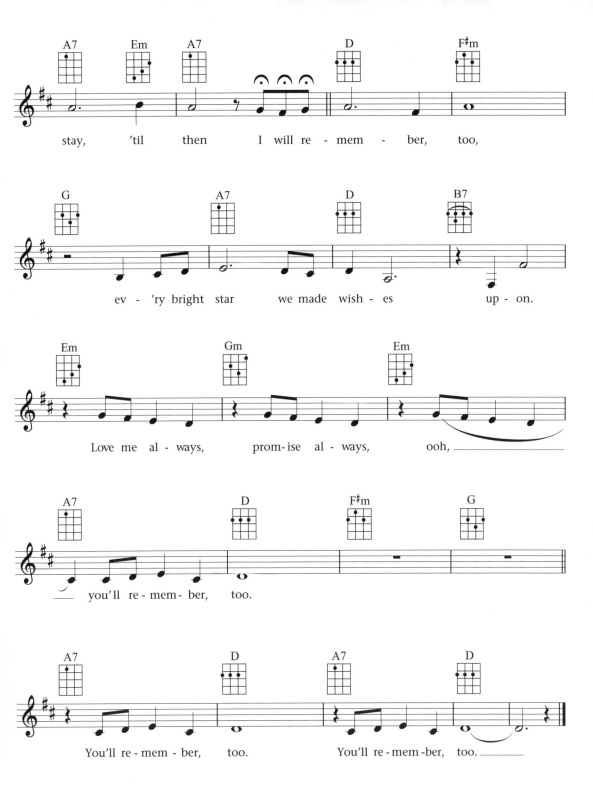

stay, 'til then I will re - mem - ber, too,

ev - 'ry bright star we made wish - es up - on.

Love me al - ways, prom - ise al - ways, ooh, _____

_____ you'll re - mem - ber, too.

You'll re - mem - ber, too. You'll re - mem - ber, too. _____

The Waikiki Beachboys

Long before there were Brian Wilson and the Beach Boys, there were the beachboys of Waikiki. Especially during the first half of the 1900s, these fun-loving, uke-strumming men of the ocean turned Hawaii's famed Waikiki Beach into their playground.

The glory days of the Waikiki beachboys mirror the development of Waikiki as a tourist destination. As the big hotels like the Moana (1901) and famous pink Royal Hawaiian (1927) opened, travelers started arriving in greater numbers looking for fun in the sun. More than happy to assist was a group of men with colorful nicknames like Chick, Turkey Love, Scooter Boy, Steamboat, Freckles, Splash and the legendary "Duke" Kahanamoku, many of whom were hugely talented swimmers, surfers and musicians. In fact, one of these beach-

boys, John "Hawkshaw" Paia, would take a surfboard, chair and uke into the ocean and, after catching a wave, would place the chair on the board and strum in it all the way back to shore. Some of the beachboys were employed by the hotels to provide surfing instruction and outrigger canoe rides during the day and to play music in the evening. Others provided similar entertainment but worked entirely for tips.

Some were known as heroic men of the ocean and of these beachboys none was more famous than Duke Kahanamoku (1890-1968). He was an extraordinary swimmer who competed in four Olympic Games and won five medals. He is also credited with introducing surfing to the world. During the late teens, he played a major role in popularizing surfing on both coasts of the United States. In his later years, during the 1960s, Duke began putting his name on lines of clothing, surfboards and ukuleles. Today you can see a majestic statue of the Duke on the beach at Waikiki. Though it may be larger than the man was in reality, for many it represents his enormous contributions to Hawaii as an athlete, goodwill ambassador and beachboy.

*Courtesy of Cord
International Archive*

Duke Kahanamoku, 1930
Photo by Tai Sing Loo

Surf Polo at Waikiki Beach in front of the
Royal Hawaiian Hotel, 1920s
Hawaii State Archives

Love Letters In The Sand

Words by
NICK & CHARLES KENNY

Music by
J. FRED COOTS

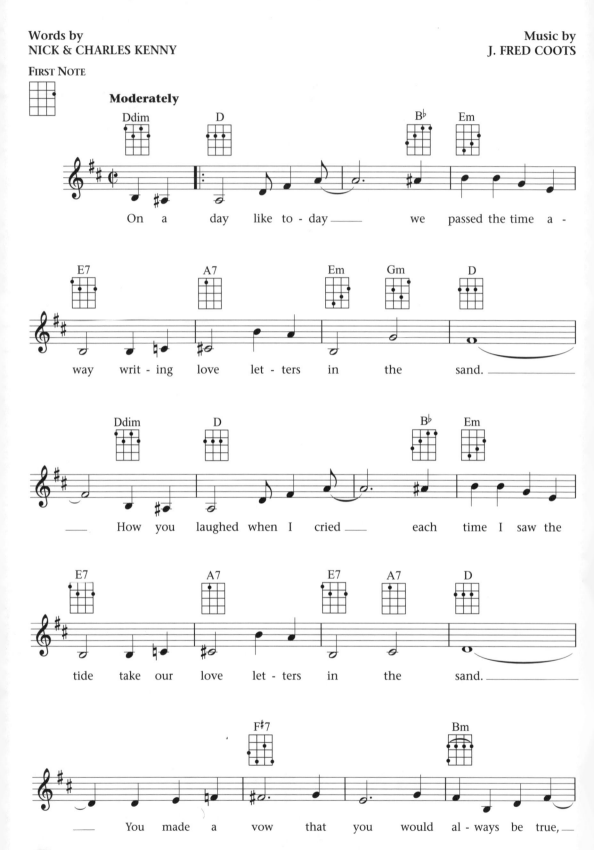

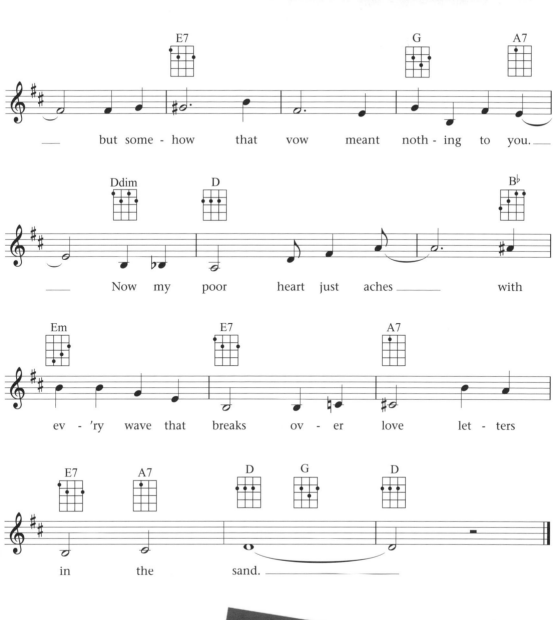

but some - how that vow meant noth - ing to you.

Now my poor heart just aches _____ with

ev - 'ry wave that breaks ov - er love let - ters

in the sand. _____

"Some of the happy musical moments of my life have been accompanied by my own flying fingers on a baritone uke."

—Pat Boone

PAT BOONE

Pineapple Princess

Words and Music by
RICHARD M. SHERMAN and
ROBERT B. SHERMAN

FIRST NOTE

Pine - ap - ple Prin - cess, he calls me, Pine - ap - ple
Prin - cess all day, as he plays his uk - u - le - le on the
hill a - bove the bay. Pine - ap - ple Prin - cess, I
love you, you're the sweet - est girl I've seen. Some -
day we're gon - na mar - ry and you'll be my Pine - ap - ple

Queen!

1. I saw a boy on O-ah-u Isle, float-ing down the bay on a croc-o-dile. He waved at me as he swam a-shore, and I knew he'd be mine for-ev-er more. _____ Pine-ap-ple

2. He sings his song on from ba-na-na trees, he e-ven sings to me on his wa-ter skis. We went skin-div-ing and be-neath the blue, he sang and played the uk-u-le-le too. _____ Pine-ap-ple

3. We'll set-tle down in a bam-boo hut, and he will be my own lit-tle co-co-nut. Then we'll be beach-comb-ing roy-al-ty, on wick-y wick-y, wack-y Wai-ki-ki. _____ Pine-ap-ple

Rock-A-Hula Baby

Words and Music by
FRED WISE, BEN WEISMAN,
and DOLORES FULLER

1. The way she moves her hips up to her fin - ger - tips, I feel I'm heaven bound. And when she starts to sway I've got - ta say, she real - ly moves the grass a - round.
2. love to kiss my lit - tle hu - la miss, I nev - er get the chance. I wan - na hold her tight all through the night, but all she wants to do is dance.
3. she could teach the palms a - long the beach to sway when breez - es blow. And birds up in the sky could learn to fly by watch - in' how my ba - by can go.

Rock a - hu - la ba - by, rock

F   C

a - hu - la ba - by. Got a hu - la lu - lu from

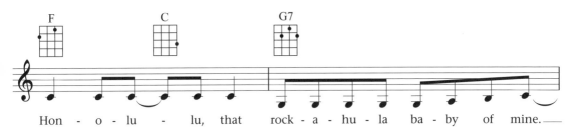

F   C   G7

Hon - o - lu - lu, that rock - a - hu - la ba - by of mine.____

1., 2. C   3. C

____   2. Al - though I   ____
                                3. I   bet   that

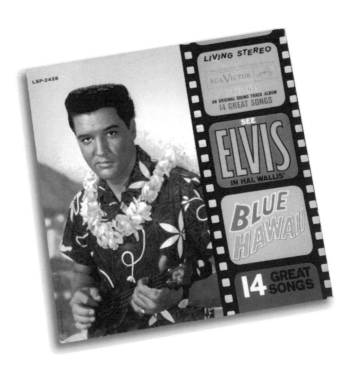

Misirlou

Music by
NICOLAS ROUBANIS

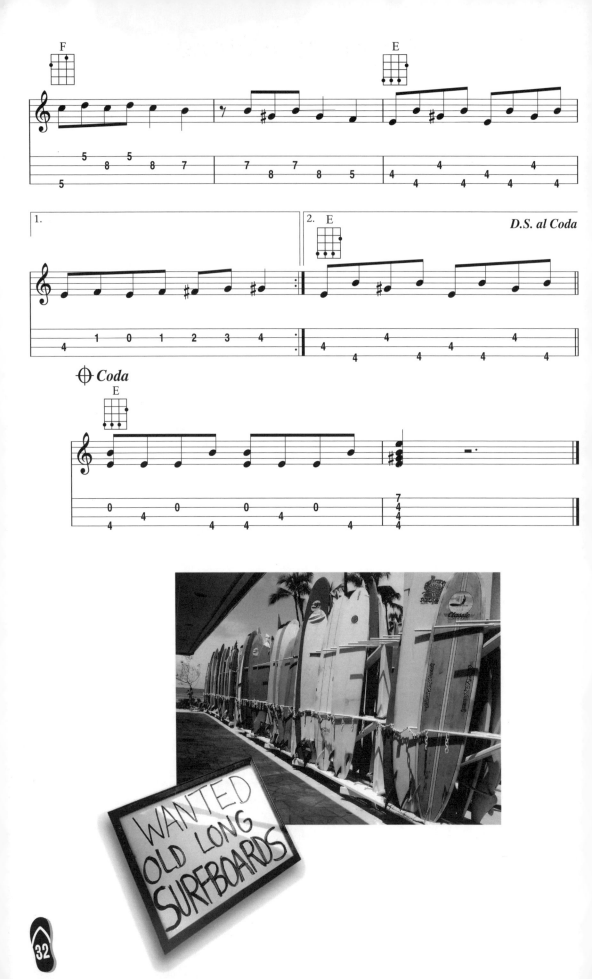

A Summer Place

Words by
MACK DISCANT

Music by
MAX STEINER

FIRST NOTE

Dreamily

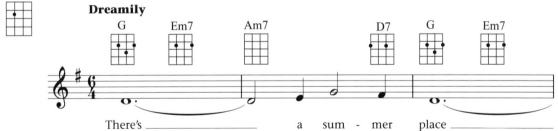

There's _____ a sum - mer place _____

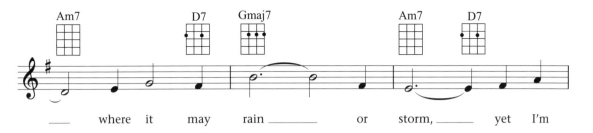

_____ where it may rain _____ or storm, _____ yet I'm

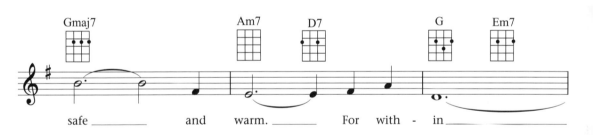

safe _____ and warm. _____ For with - in _____

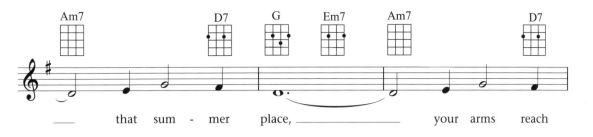

_____ that sum - mer place, _____ your arms reach

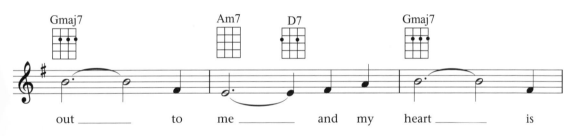

out _____ to me _____ and my heart _____ is

33

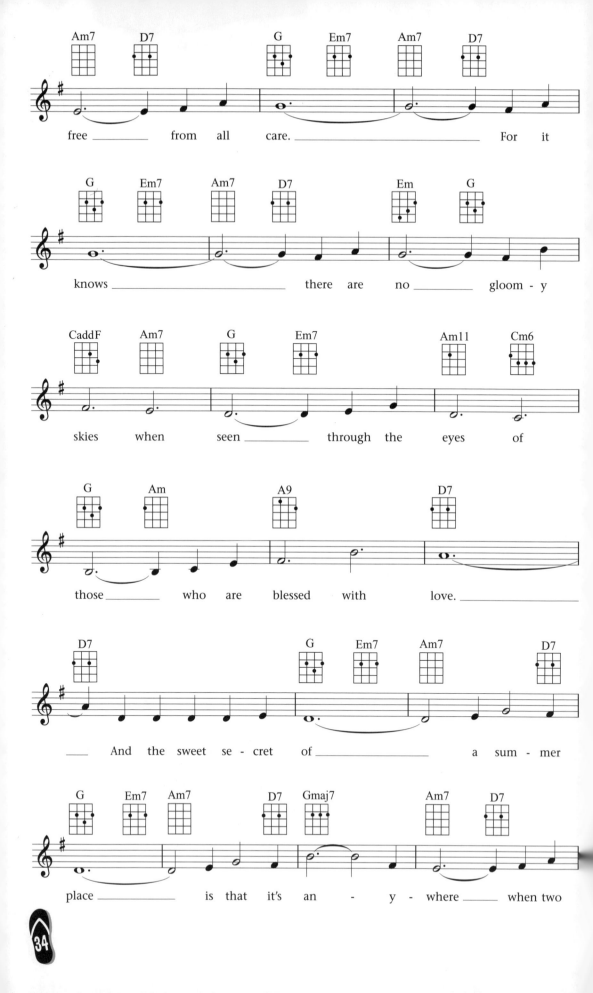

free _____ from all care. _____ For it

knows _____ there are no _____ gloom - y

skies when seen _____ through the eyes of

those _____ who are blessed with love. _____

____ And the sweet se - cret of _____ a sum - mer

place _____ is that it's an - y - where _____ when two

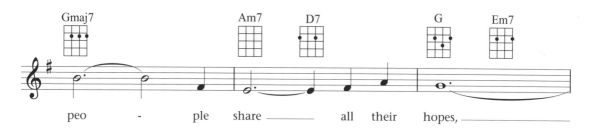

peo - ple share _____ all their hopes, _____

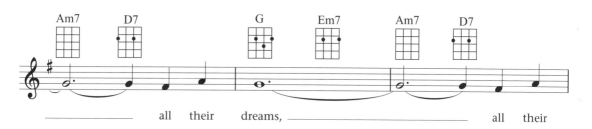

_____ all their dreams, _____ all their

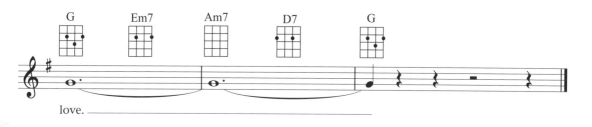

love. _____

Surf City

Words and Music by
BRIAN WILSON and JAN BERRY

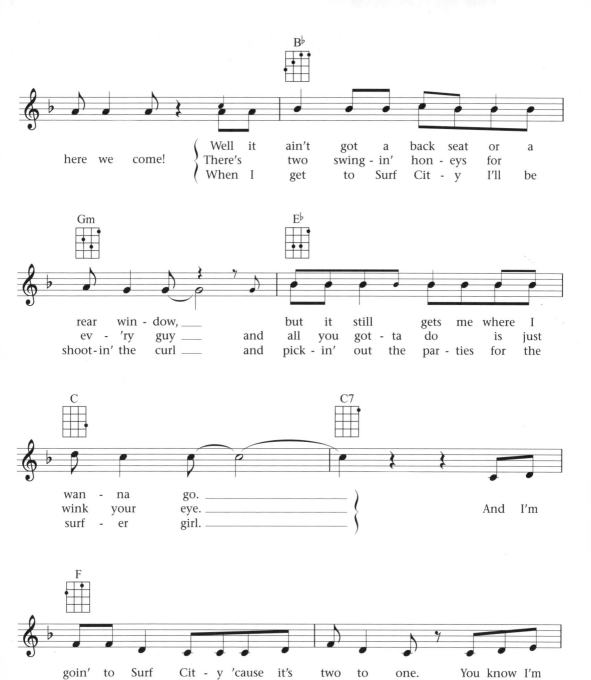

here we come!

Well it ain't got a back seat or a
There's two swing-in' hon-eys for
When I get to Surf Cit-y I'll be

rear win-dow, ___ but it still gets me where I
ev-'ry guy ___ and all you got-ta do is just
shoot-in' the curl ___ and pick-in' out the par-ties for the

wan - na go. ___
wink your eye. ___
surf - er girl. ___

And I'm

goin' to Surf Cit-y 'cause it's two to one. You know I'm

goin' to Surf Cit-y, gon-na have some fun. Yeah, I'm

goin' to Surf Cit - y 'cause it's two to one. You know I'm

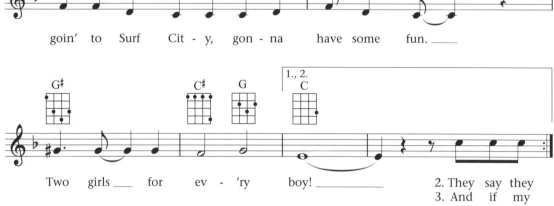

goin' to Surf Cit - y, gon - na have some fun. _____

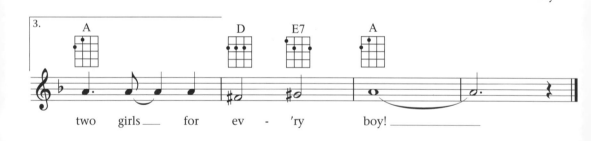

Two girls _____ for ev - 'ry boy! _____

2. They say they
3. And if my

two girls _____ for ev - 'ry boy! _____

The Hawaiian Surf Club of San Onofre

Surfin' Safari

Words and Music by
BRIAN WILSON and MIKE LOVE

FIRST NOTE

Let's go surf-in' now, ev-'ry-bod-y's learn-in' how,

come on a sa-fa-ri with me._____

1. Ear-ly in the morn-in' we'll be
2. ang-lin' in La-gu-na and

start-in' out,_____ some hon-eys will be com-in' a-long._____
Cerro A-zul,_____ they're kick-in' out in Do-he-ny too._____

___ We're load-in' up our Wood-y with the
___ I tell you surf-in's run-nin' wild, it's get-tin'

boards in-side and head-in' out sing-in' our song._____
big-ger ev-'ry day from Ha-wai-i to the shores of Pe-ru._____

39

D

Come on, ba - by, wait and see, ___ yes,

G

I'm gon - na take you surf - in' with me. ___ Lone-some ba - by,

D

wait and see, ___ yes, I'm gon - na take you surf - in' with me. ___

A   G

Let's go surf - in' now, ev - 'ry - bod - y's learn - in' how;

E7   A7

come on a sa - fa - ri with me. ___ In

D   G

Hunt - ing - ton and Ma - li - bu they're shoot - in' the pier, ___ in

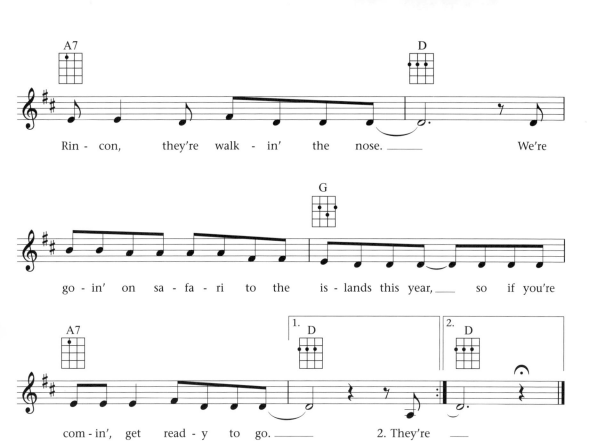

Rin - con, they're walk - in' the nose. _____ We're

go - in' on sa - fa - ri to the is - lands this year, _____ so if you're

A7 ... **1. D** ... **2. D**

com - in', get read - y to go. _____ 2. They're _____

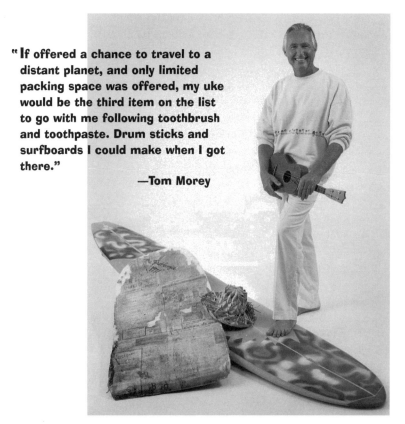

" **If offered a chance to travel to a distant planet, and only limited packing space was offered, my uke would be the third item on the list to go with me following toothbrush and toothpaste. Drum sticks and surfboards I could make when I got there.** "

—**Tom Morey**

Tom Morey (aka Y), inventor of the Boogie Board, surfer and uke player since 1947.

Sand In My Shoes

Words and Music by
JIM BELOFF

blues _____ and the __ sand _____ in my

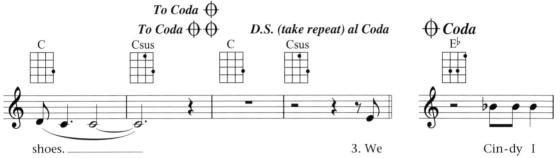

shoes. _____ 3. We Cin-dy I

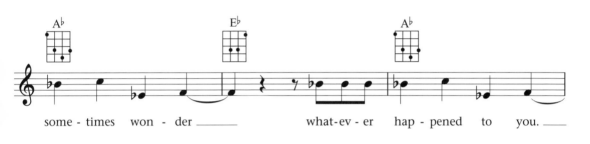

some-times won-der _____ what-ev-er hap-pened to you. __

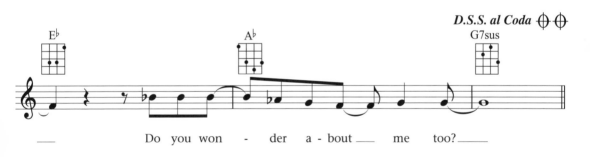

__ Do you won - der a-bout __ me too? _____

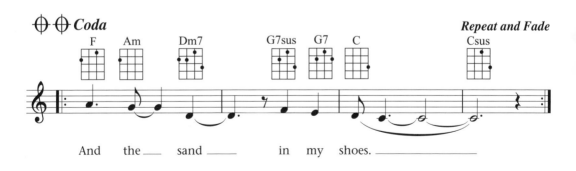

And the __ sand _____ in my shoes. _____

43

A Summer Song

Words and Music by CLIVE METCALFE,
KEITH NOBLE and DAVID STUART

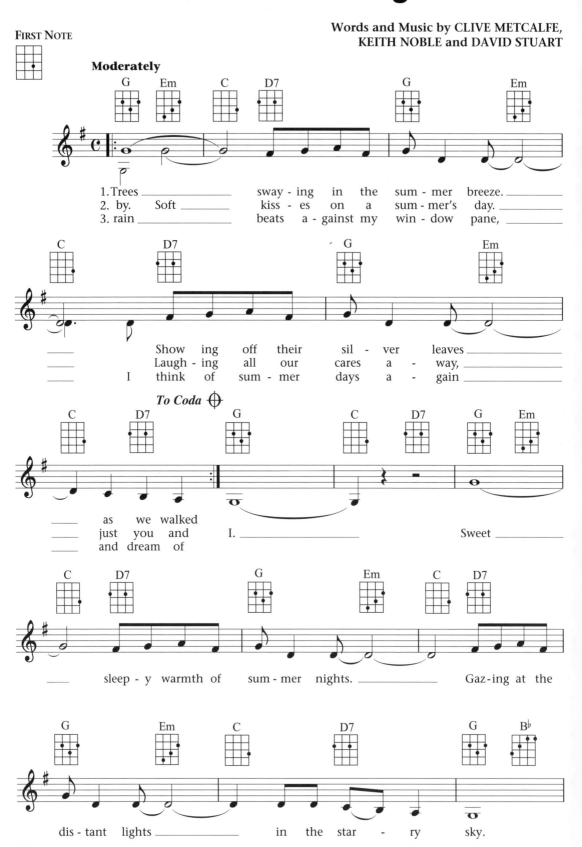

1. Trees ____ sway-ing in the sum-mer breeze. ____
2. by. Soft ____ kiss-es on a sum-mer's day. ____
3. rain ____ beats a-gainst my win-dow pane, ____

____ Show-ing off their sil-ver leaves ____
____ Laugh-ing all our cares a-way, ____
____ I think of sum-mer days a-gain ____

To Coda ⊕

____ as we walked ____
____ just you and I. ____ Sweet ____
____ and dream of

____ sleep-y warmth of sum-mer nights. ____ Gaz-ing at the

____ dis-tant lights ____ in the star-ry sky.

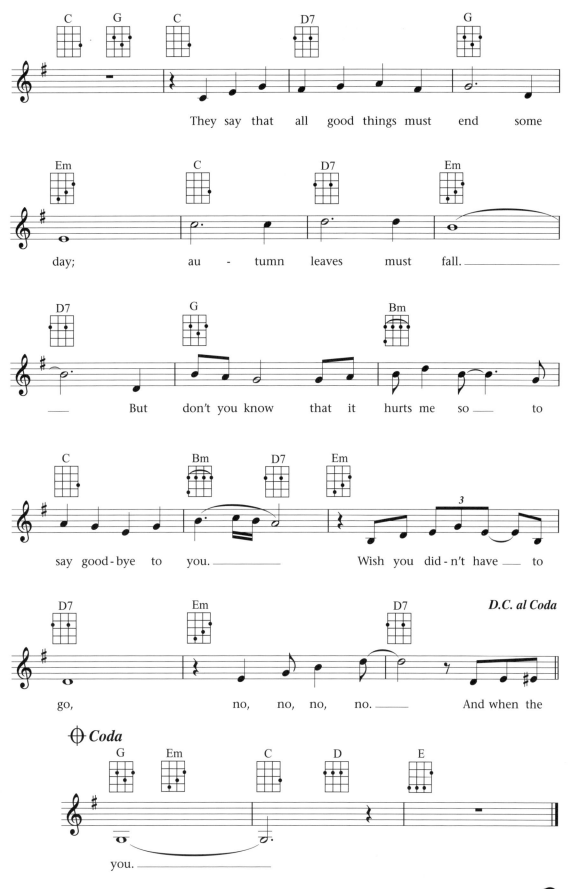

They say that all good things must end some day; au - tumn leaves must fall. But don't you know that it hurts me so to say good - bye to you. Wish you did - n't have to go, no, no, no, no. And when the

⊕ Coda

you.

Surfer Girl

Words and Music by
BRIAN WILSON

1. Lit - tle surf - er, lit - tle one,
2. I have watched you on the shore,

made my heart come all un - done. Do you love me,
stand - ing by the o - cean's roar. Do you love me,

do you, surf - er girl?
do you, surf - er girl?

We could ride the surf to - geth - er

while our love would grow. In my Wood - y

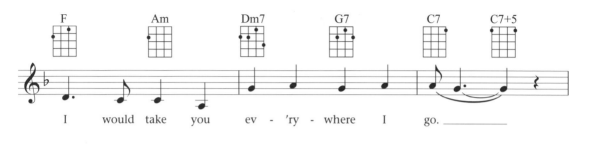

I would take you ev - 'ry - where I go. _____

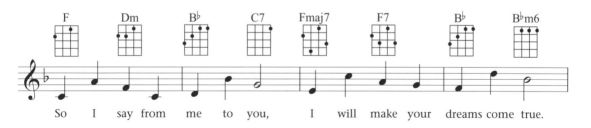

So I say from me to you, I will make your dreams come true.

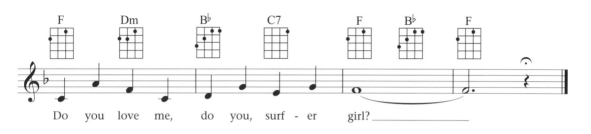

Do you love me, do you, surf - er girl? _____

The Things We Did Last Summer

Words by
SAMMY CAHN

Music by
JULE STYNE

The boat rides we would take, the moon-light on the lake, the way we danced and hummed our fav-'rite song, the things we did last sum-mer, I'll re-mem-ber all win-ter long. The mid-way and the fun, the kew-pie dolls we won, the bell { I you } rang to prove that { I you } { was were } strong, the things we did last

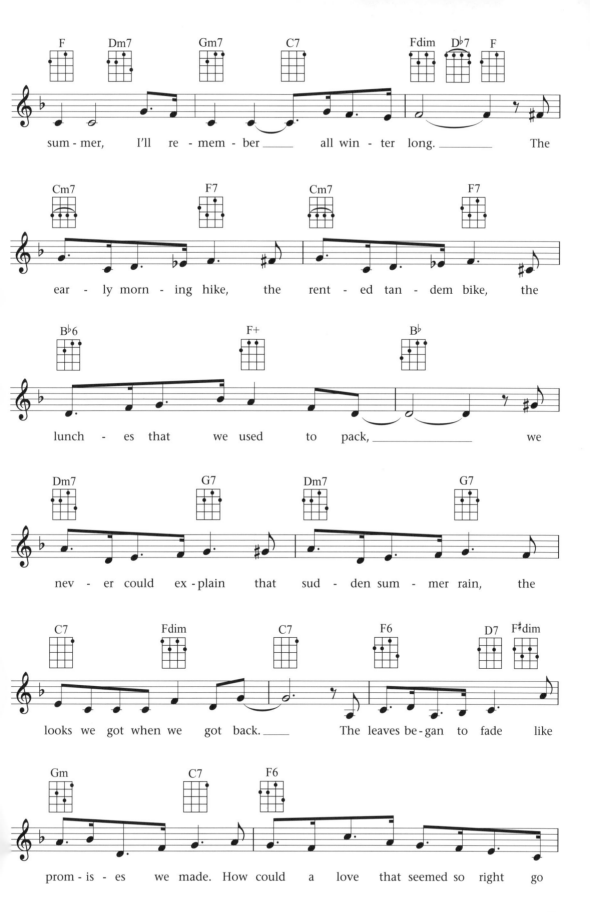

sum - mer, I'll re - mem - ber _____ all win - ter long. _____ The

ear - ly morn - ing hike, the rent - ed tan - dem bike, the

lunch - es that we used to pack, _____ we

nev - er could ex - plain that sud - den sum - mer rain, the

looks we got when we got back. _____ The leaves be - gan to fade like

prom - is - es we made. How could a love that seemed so right go

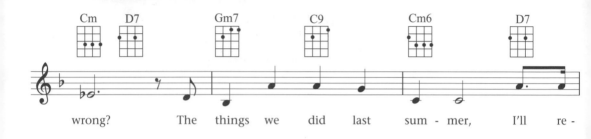

wrong? The things we did last sum - mer, I'll re -

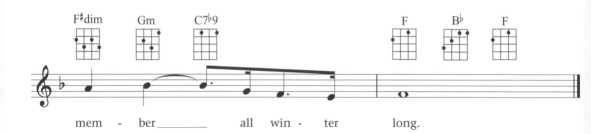

mem - ber _____ all win - ter long.

*Ian Whitcomb,
strumming on
Malibu Beach in the
TV show, "Where
The Action Is."*

IAN WHITCOMB
July 1966

26 Miles
(Santa Catalina)

Words and Music by
GLEN LARSON and BRUCE BELLAND

FIRST NOTE

Moderate Rock Tempo

Twen-ty-six miles a - cross the sea, San-ta Cat-a-li-na is a-

wait-in' for me, San-ta Cat-a-li-na, the is-land of ro-mance,

ro-mance, romance, ro-mance. Wa-ter all a-round it ev-'ry-where,

trop-i-cal trees and the salt-y air, but for me the thing that's a-

wait-in' there's ro-mance. It seems so dis-tant,
A trop-i-cal hea-ven

26 Miles (Santa Catalina)
Additional verse by Bruce Belland
(Special ukulele version dedicated to my friend Jim Beloff)

```
                     G      Em   Am     D7
(Verse)   Twenty-six miles across the sea,
                     G      Em         Am       D7
          my lovely ukulele lady's waitin' for me.
                     G            Em              Am        D7
          'Cause each and every time she hears "My Dog Has Fleas,"
                     G      Em  Am   D7
          it sends her into ecstasy.


                     G            Em           Am   D7
(Verse)   Guys and their guitars can get to be a bore,
                     G        Em           Am       D7
          especially when you're lovin' on the Avalon shore.
                     G         Em            Am       D7   G  Em Am  D7
          You'll find a uke is always more convenient for... romance.


                     C6         D9        G          Em7
(Bridge)  My four-string friend has always been there for me.
                     Am            D9             G  G7
          It's been my buddy right from the start.
                     C6          D9          G         Em7
          It's always come through when I need a melody.
                     A7                    D7
          That's why I hold it near my heart.


                     G      Em         Am    D7
(Verse)   So ukulele lovers of the world unite!
                     G      Em         Am     D7
          Take a uke along on your date tonight,
                     G            Em           Am          D7
          'cause with some lucky pluckin' there's no lady who'll fight...
                     G      Em    Am      D7
          romance, romance, romance, romance.
```

The Story Behind "26 Miles"

On a sweltering August day in the late '50s, I cut my summer school class at Hollywood High and headed for the beach with my buddies. That afternoon, flaked out on the sand, one of the guys pointed out Catalina in the distance and speculated that it was "around 26 miles" away.

I picked up my ukulele (which was a definite "chick magnet" for a beach Lothario back then) and began to compose a song called "26 Miles" that would ultimately take my high school recording group, the Four Preps, to dizzying heights and put my kids through school.

I was recently honored with a certificate from BMI saluting the one millionth performance of the song and over the years "26 Miles" has been cited by musical figures like Brian Wilson as one of his high school favorites and made such an impression on a teen-aged Jimmy Buffett that he named a chapter after it in his recent best-selling autobiography.

Not bad for a song written by a high school truant who only knew three chords and had never been to the island at the time!

Bruce Belland
Encino, California

Surfin' U.S.A.

Words and Music by
CHUCK BERRY

You'll catch 'em surf - in' at Del Mar,
At Hag - gar - ty's and Swam - i's,

Ven - tur - a Coun - try Line, San - ta Cruz and Tress - els,
Pac - if - ic Pal - i - sades, San O - no - fre and Sun - set,

Aus - tra - lia's Nar - a - bine., all o - ver Man -
Re - don - do Beach, L. A., all o - ver La

hat - tan and down Do - he - ny way.
Joll - a, at Wai - a - me - a Bay.

Ev - 'ry - bod - y's gone surf - in', surf - in' U. S. A.
Ev - 'ry - bod - y's gone surf - in', surf - in' U. S. A.

1.
We'll all be plan - nin' out a

2.

Sweet Someone

Words by
GEORGE WAGGNER

Music by
BARON KEYES

Sweet some - one, who - ev - er you may be; sweet some - one, you suit me to a "T." Al - though you pay no at - ten - tion to me at all; one kiss and need - less to men - tion I had to fall.

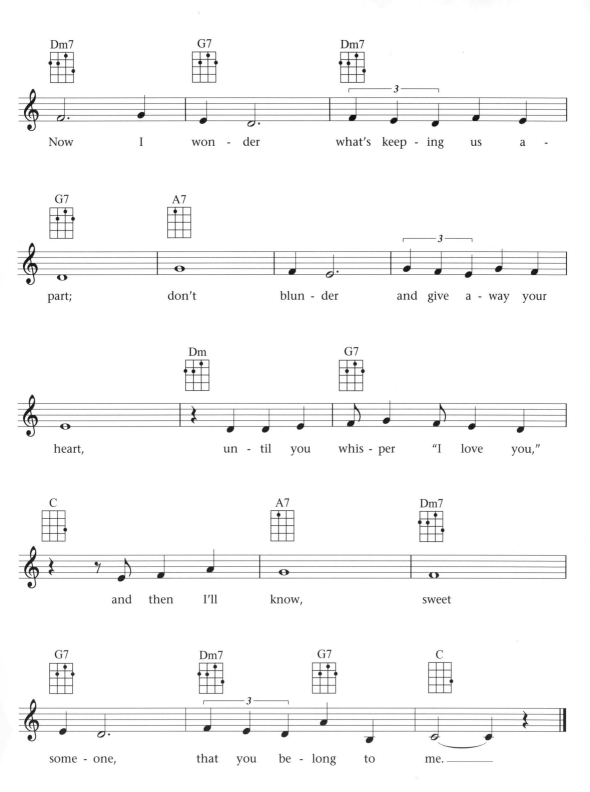

Now   I   won - der   what's keep - ing   us   a -

part;   don't   blun - der   and give a - way your

heart,   un - til you   whis - per   "I   love   you,"

and   then   I'll   know,   sweet

some - one,   that   you   be - long   to   me. _____

Those Lazy-Hazy-Crazy Days Of Summer

Words and Music by
CHARLES TOBIAS and HANS CARSTE

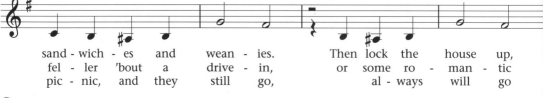

Under The Boardwalk

Words and Music by
ARTIE RESNICK and KENNY YOUNG

Moderately, with a Beat

Oh, when the 1. sun beats down — and burns the
2. park you hear — the hap - py

tar up - on the roof, ___ and your
sound of a car - ou - sel, ___ you can

shoes get so hot you wish your tired feet ___ were fire -
al - most taste the hot - dogs and french - fries ___

- proof. Un - der the board - walk, ___
they sell. Un - der the board - walk, ___

down by the sea, ___ yeah, on a
down by the sea, ___ yeah, on a

blan - ket with my   ba - by's _____   where I'll _____ be. _____
blan - ket with my   ba - by's _____   where I'll _____ be. _____

(Un - der the   board - walk)   Out   of   the   sun _____ (Un - der the

board - walk)   we'll   be   hav - in'   some   fun. _____   (Un - der   the

board - walk)   Peo - ple   walk - in'   a - bove _____   (Un - der   the

we'll   be   fall - in'   in   love _____   un - der   the
board - walk)   (Un - der   the

1.
board - walk,   board - walk.   From   the
board - walk,   board - walk.)

2.
walk.

The Kooky-Ukes

From the Surfing Coast of Southern California

Part of the ongoing charm of the ukulele is how well it seems to accommodate offbeat designs. Some of the most outlandish ukuleles came from Ancil Swagerty who created the Surf-A-Lele, the Kook-a-lā-lee, and the Trēhōlipee. Born in 1911 in New Mexico, Swagerty started his professional life as a rodeo clown. Subsequent career moves included cattle ranching, gold mining, and flying planes during the war. He also had a strong creative side that led him into architecture, furniture building and contracting. In 1952, Swagerty moved to San Clemente, California. While working in the lumber business in 1964, he hand-built an oddly shaped musical instrument that he thought might make an interesting piece of wall art. A friend wondered if it might be made to play, and the two of them worked on a model that could. The result of this was the three sound hole Trēhōlipee, a 4½ foot long creature with a long neck and paddle-shaped tuners that played like a uke. Amazingly it sounded better and played more easily than one would expect.

From 1964 to 1967, Swagerty Specialties Company sold an estimated 60,000 Kooky-Ukes. Trēhōlipees sold for $19.95, Kook-a-lā-lees for $17.95 and Surf-A-Leles for $13.95. Big national department stores such as Sears and the May Co. took them in as did many Southern California music stores. None other than Steve Allen endorsed the line of Kooky-Ukes and a hang tag proclaimed "Steve Allen Presents The Kooky-Ukes From The Surfing Coast Of Southern California. A New Sound For A New Generation." The Kooky-Ukes also came in a hip assortment of colors including, "Breaker Blue," "Stoked Orange," "All Time Sand," and "Hot Doggin' Pink" for the Surf-A-Lele and "County Orange," "Clemente Brown," "California Gold," "Fiesta Red," and "Capistrano Olive" for the Kook-a-lā-lee and the Trēhōlipee. For pop culture archaeologists, the Swagerty ukes also incorporated a cool Rick Griffin cartoon of a surfer shooting a curl and strumming his Kooky-Uke. Promotional photos at the time include Jack Benny, Dick Van Dyke, Carl Reiner, "Country" Washburne, as well as Steve Allen, all clowning around with their Kooky-Ukes.

Ancil Swagerty

On all of the promotional materials for Kooky-Ukes, Swagerty proudly listed his company's address as "Main Offices in Beautiful San Clemente (By the Sea), California." The ocean connection was important. When at the beach, both the Trēhōlipee and Kook-a-lā-lee had an extra long end that could be stuck in the sand when not in use, and the shorter Surf-A-Lele was designed to be played while riding on a surfboard. Apparently, all the Kooky-Ukes were water resistant.

Like many fads of the day, the Kooky-Ukes had their moment and then passed on into ukulele history. Nonetheless, Ancil Swagerty's attitude toward them was timeless. In the Kooky-Uke "How To" songbook he wrote, "You don't have to be a surfer to play these aquatic gizmos or even live near the ocean. All you need are a few fingers, one foot to pat, and an old conch shell to listen to the sound of the surf. So here you go, relax and have fun."

FUN TO PLAY

Steve Allen

From The Surfing Coast of Southern California

The Surf·A·Lele

The Trēhōlipee

The Kook·a·lā·Lee

A new Sound for A new Generation

63

Where The Boys Are

Words and Music by
HOWARD GREENFIELD
and NEIL SEDAKA

FIRST NOTE

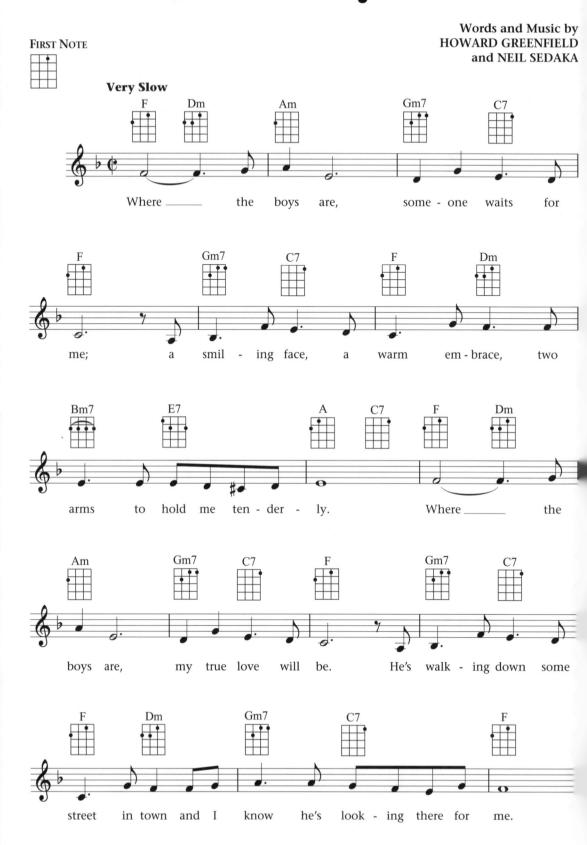

Wipe Out

By
The Surfaris

Twangy Rock Beat

(Tap drum beat on uke during breaks—Go wild!)

Wouldn't It Be Nice

Words and Music by
BRIAN WILSON, TONY ASHER
and MIKE LOVE

Would - n't it be nice if we were old -
nice if we could wake

er, ___ then ___ we would - n't have to wait ___ so ___
___ up ___ in ___ the morn - ing when the day ___ is ___

long. ___ And would - n't it be nice to live to - geth -
new. ___ And af - ter that to spend the day to - geth -

er ___ in ___ the kind of world where we'd ___ be - long. ___
er, ___ hold ___ each oth - er close the whole ___ night ___ through. ___

Though it's gon - na make it that much ___ bet - ter ___
The hap - py times to - geth - er we'd been ___ spend - ing, ___

when we can say good-night and stay to-geth - er.____
I wish that ev - 'ry kiss was nev - er-end - ing. ____

1. C9   **2.** C9   C11   F

Would-n't it be   Oh would-n't it ___ be ___ nice. ____

D   G

Well, may-be if ___ we think and wish and hope and pray it
Ba - by, then ___ there would-n't be a sin - gle thing we

F♯m   **1.** Bm7   **2.** Bm7

might come ___ true. ____
could - n't ___ do. ____   We ___ could be mar -

F♯m7   Bm7   F♯m7

ried _____   and then we'd be hap - py. ____

C9   C11   F

____ Oh, would-n't it ___ be ___ nice. ____

See You In September

Words by
SID WAYNE

Music by
SHERMAN EDWARDS

I'll be a - lone each and ev - 'ry night.

While you're a - way, don't for - get to write. See you ___

___ in Sep - tem - ber, ___ see you ___

___ when the sum - mer's through. ___ Here we are,

say - ing good - bye at the sta - tion, ___ sum - mer va - ca - tion ___

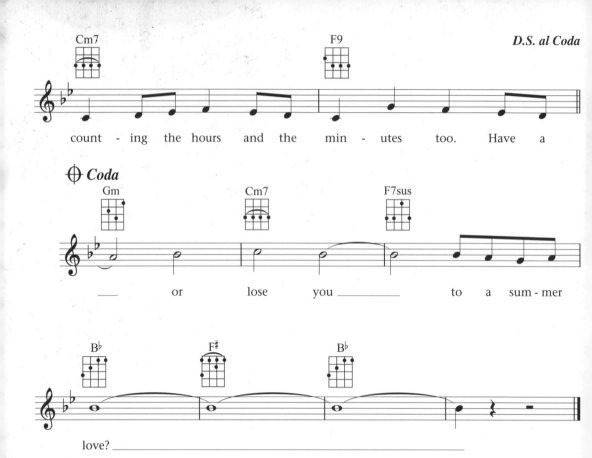

Cm7   F9

count - ing the hours and the min - utes too. Have a

⊕ *Coda*

Gm   Cm7   F7sus

____ or lose you _____ to a sum - mer

B♭   F♯   B♭

love? _____